D0277145

NEWCASTLE-UNDER-LYME
COLLEGE LEARNING RESOURCES

Newcastle Under Lyme College

DC035945

NEWCASTLE UNDER LYME
COLLEGE LEARNING RESOURCES

LIFE SKILLS

MANAGING MONEY

Barbara Hollander

332.024
NEWCASTLE-UNDER-LYME
COLLEGE LEARNING RESOURCES
DC035945

Heinemann
LIBRARY

www.heinemann.co.uk/library

Visit our website to find out more information about **Heinemann Library** books.

To order:

☎ Phone 44 (0) 1865 888066

🖹 Send a fax to 44 (0) 1865 314091

💻 Visit the Heinemann Bookshop at www.heinemann.co.uk/library to browse our catalogue and order online.

Heinemann Library is an imprint of **Pearson Education Limited**, a company incorporated in England and Wales having its registered office at Edinburgh Gate, Harlow, Essex, CM20 2JE – Registered company number: 00872828

"Heinemann" is a registered trademark of Pearson Education Limited.

Text © Pearson Education Limited 2009
First published in hardback in 2009
The moral rights of the proprietor have been asserted.

All rights reserved. No part of this publication may be reproduced in any form or by any means (including photocopying or storing it in any medium by electronic means and whether or not transiently or incidentally to some other use of this publication) without the written permission of the copyright owner, except in accordance with the provisions of the Copyright, Designs and Patents Act 1988 or under the terms of a licence issued by the Copyright Licensing Agency, Saffron House, 6–10 Kirby Street, London EC1N 8TS (www.cla.co.uk). Applications for the copyright owner's written permission should be addressed to the Publisher.

Edited by Harriet Milles
Designed by Philippa Jenkins and Hart MacLeod
Original illustrations © Pearson Education Limited by Clare Elsom
Picture research by Elizabeth Alexander and Maria Joannou
Production by Alison Parsons
Originated by Modern Age Repro House Ltd.
Printed and bound in China by South China Printing Company Ltd.

ISBN 978 0 431112343
13 12 11 10 09
10 9 8 7 6 5 4 3 2 1

British Library Cataloguing-in-Publication Data
Hollander, Barbara
  Managing money. - (Life skills)
  1. Finance, Personal - Juvenile literature
  I. Title
  332'.024

Acknowledgements
We would like to thank the following for permission to reproduce photographs: ©Alamy **pp. 11** (Image Source Black), **25** (vario images GmbH & Co.KG), **13** (Angela Hampton Picture Library), **47** (Blend Images), **39** (David J. Green—Lifestyle), **44** (Rob Bartee); ©Bridgeman Art Library/Private Collection **p. 8**; ©Corbis **pp. 31**, **34** (Alan Schein Photography), **4** (JLP/Jose L. Pelaez), **49** (Randy Faris); ©Getty Images **pp. 7** (Issouf Sanogo), **37** (The Image Bank); ©Photographers Direct/Jim Worlding, Reality Images **p. 29**; ©Photolibrary **pp. 20** (Photononstop/Charlie Abad), **10** (Poplis Paul), **42** (Steve Vidler), **19** (Image Source); ©Rex Features/ Garo/Phanie **p. 15**.

Cover photograph of a man with empty pockets reproduced with permission of ©Corbis/ Hill Street Studios/Brand X.

We would like to thank John Pueck for his invaluable help in the preparation of this book.

Every effort has been made to contact copyright holders of material reproduced in this book. Any omissions will be rectified in subsequent printings if notice is given to the Publishers.

Contents

Some words are printed in bold, **like this**. You can find out
what they mean by looking in the glossary.

A Brief History of Money

Imagine that you lived 400 years ago and you only knew how to bake bread. You ate bread for breakfast, lunch, and dinner. But one day you felt like eating something else. So you packed several loaves and began walking down the street. After an hour, you came to a man who had a basket of apples. You swapped, or traded, your bread for his apples. Before the existence of money, this system of **bartering** was used to acquire goods and services.

A System of Bartering

Long ago, people bartered their goods for things they **needed** or **wanted**. The word barter comes from the French word "*barater*," which means "to trade".

When small children swap snacks with their friends, they are bartering.

Many goods and services were used for bartering. Neighbours traded animals and crops. Blacksmiths, who make things from iron, travelled to fairs to trade their wares for food. People even traded services, such as helping to build a house.

International bartering

Bartering also occurred between people in different countries. For example, over 1,000 years ago Europeans took furs and crafts to the East and traded them for silk and spices. Bartering allowed people to acquire goods and services, even from faraway places.

Bartering problems

Although bartering was a widely used practice, it presented several problems. People were not always willing to trade their goods for available items. It was also difficult to agree on a fair price. Often, two people had different ideas about what their goods were worth. For example, an apple grower might think that one basket of apples is worth two baskets of oranges, but the orange seller might think that one basket of apples is worth one basket of oranges.

As time went on, bartering grew more complicated, and so people searched for other ways to acquire goods and services. Today, there is something that allows people to buy food, clothes, and even CDs more easily – MONEY!

DID YOU KNOW?

In the early 1800s, Meriwether Lewis and William Clark set out to explore the western part of the present-day United States. This famous journey was called the Lewis and Clark Expedition. Here is a journal entry from their trip:

24 August 1805

As the Indians who were on their way down the Missouri had a number of spare horses with them, I thought it probable that I could obtain some of them and therefore desired the chief to speak to them and inform me whether they would trade . . . I soon purchased three horses and a mule in exchange for axes and knives.

Yesterday's money

What do shells, teeth, salt, and limestone have in common? They were all once used for money! Easy to carry or valuable items were popular choices for **currency**.

Commodity money

Throughout history different cultures have used different forms of currency. Many earlier forms of money were **commodities**. The value of commodity money is represented by the actual goods.

- In 1200 BCE the Chinese used cowrie shells. These small white shells are found in the Pacific and Indian Oceans. In the 1950s cowrie shells were still used as money in parts of Africa. That makes cowrie shells the longest-used currency in history!
- On the island of Fiji, in the South Pacific Ocean, whales' teeth once bought goods and services.
- In Papua New Guinea, in the southwestern Pacific Ocean, dogs' teeth were once the country's currency.
- At one time salt was considered a precious commodity all over the world. Until the 1920s Ethiopians, who live in eastern Africa, used salt for money. Our word salary means money earned by working. This word reflects the use of salt as currency – salary literally means "given salt".

DID YOU KNOW?

The Oldest Money

The first form of money was livestock, including cows, sheep, and oxen. Between 9000 and 6000 BCE people used cattle as commodity money. Many early coins even have pictures of cattle on them. For example, the oldest Greek coin features an ox. In the 1900s cattle were still used as commodity money in parts of Africa.

- On the island of Yap, in the Pacific Ocean, people valued limestone. They travelled to a nearby island and brought back the stones in their canoes. The value of a limestone disc was determined both by its size and by the danger of the journey. Limestone money was very hard to carry, as it was quite heavy!

Another precious commodity was cacao beans, which are used to make chocolate.

A Tasty Currency

What does chocolate have to do with money? The answer is in the cacao bean. Cacao beans are used to make chocolate. Long ago, hot chocolate was the most popular drink in the Aztec Empire in Mexico (1325–1521). Because the Aztecs believed that chocolate was the drink of the gods, cacao beans were considered precious and valuable. The beans became a form of commodity money. So for the Aztecs, money really did grow on trees!

TODAY'S MONEY

Today, the currency used by most countries consists of coins and paper money. The earliest coins were probably invented around 650 BCE in Lydia (present-day Turkey). The coins, made from a mixture of gold and silver, were called electrum.

Paper money was first made in China over 2,000 years ago. The Chinese did not have a lot of metal to make coins, but they did have the printing press. The Chinese therefore printed money, and their government guaranteed that the paper money was worth a certain amount of coins.

Coins and paper money have several advantages. Both can fit in a person's pocket and are durable. They come in different **denominations** including, for example, 50p coins and £20 notes. Currencies also state their values. A £20 note has the number "20" on it.

Today's money has two purposes:

- As a medium of exchange. People can trade it for things they need or want.

- To show the value of something. Goods and services have prices attached to them. The price tells the cost of an item.

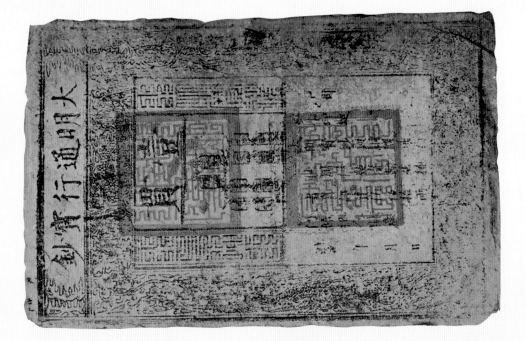

The first paper money that could be used by ordinary people was made in China during the Song dynasty (960–1279).

Minting coins

Coins are made in buildings called **mints**. They are stamped out of metals such as copper, zinc, nickel, and iron. Copper is the most popular metal for highly distributed coins. It is used to make the 1p and 2p coins. The process of minting involves working with metal: melting it, finding its correct thickness, and making it pliable (bendable). Eventually the coin's edges are raised, its rims are marked, and its sides are stamped.

Coins throughout the world have many designs on them, including rulers, buildings, and animals.

Printing money

Paper money is also called a banknote. A country's government supervises printing. In the United Kingdom, the Bank of England issues banknotes. If you've ever used a rubber stamp and ink pad, this is a very simplified version of the paper money-making process. The most popular method for making money is called **intaglio**. It consists of dipping a patterned steel plate into ink and then pressing the plate on the paper. The person who makes the steel plate is called an engraver.

Looks like money

Making paper money involves choices about colour, paper, and design. Many coloured inks are blended together to make the colour of a note. In the United Kingdom and the United States, notes are printed on paper that is a mix of cotton and linen. Banknotes in the UK also have a metallic strip running through them.

In Australia, banknotes are printed on a type of plastic called polymer. Australian money also comes in different colours and sizes. An Australian $100 green note is longer than an Australian $10 blue note. Australians can tell the value of their money at a glance.

DID YOU KNOW?

The Bank of England was established in 1694, to raise money for King William III's war against France. In return for their deposits of money, the Bank would give people a paper note stating the value of their deposit, and promising to pay back the sum on the note if they asked for it. Each note was written out by hand and signed by one of the Bank's cashiers! This is why banknotes today have printed on them: "I promise to pay the bearer on demand the sum of ..." and the signature of the Bank of England's Chief Cashier. The first fully printed banknotes were not made until 1855.

Money choices and budgets

Managing money is about meeting needs and wants. It involves understanding money choices and having a plan to achieve money **goals**.

Needs and wants

When a person says, "I need something," he or she usually means "I want something." A need is something required for survival. Food, air, and water are examples of needs. Wants are things that we would like to have. Video games, DVDs, and MP3 players are types of want. Wants often enhance our lives, but they are not absolutely necessary.

Some items, such as clothing, are both a need and a want. Obviously people need to have clothes, especially in cold climates. But they do not need 25 designer shirts or 20 pairs of boots.

What is a budget?

Should you use your spending money on a CD, or to buy lunch? Do you have money to share? How much of your pocket money should be used for **savings**? These questions are all answered with one word – **budget**.

A budget is a plan for achieving money goals. It keeps track of **income**, **expenses**, and goals.

Food is an example of both a need and a want. You need to eat, but you do not necessarily have to eat in the most expensive restaurant!

Buying a computer is an example of a money goal.

Income

Income is money that you take in. It can be:

- weekly income, including pocket money
- income received as a gift at special times, such as birthdays
- income from working, such as babysitting money.

Expenses

Expenses can be essential or non-esssential. A jumper, a CD, and school lunch are all examples of expenses. Some expenses, such as school lunch, may be **incurred** each week. Other expenses, such as spending birthday money on a video game, are incurred less regularly.

If people give up one thing in order to buy something else, this is known as the **opportunity cost**. For instance, if someone spends money on a new skirt, then that money cannot be used to pay a bill. Not paying a bill is the opportunity cost of buying the skirt.

Goals

A money goal is something that money can achieve. A short-term goal is something you may be able to achieve in a short time, such as a week or a month. A long-term goal may take a lot longer to achieve. When listing your money goals, always remember to put them in order of importance!

THE SAVER

Rose is a Saver. She is one of those people who always seems able to afford their goals – for instance, nice presents for family members' birthdays, or extra things she wants for herself. So, how does Rose do this? The answer is realistic planning and budgeting. Firstly, Rose sat down and made a list of:

- her income (weekly pocket money)
- her weekly expenses
- her long-term and short-term goals.

Rose saw that her weekly pocket money and her expenses came to the same amount (£5). The only way she could start to save was by cutting out her occasional drinks and snacks, and/or her weekly get-together with her friends.

Cutting out the drinks and snacks was possible. Rose could save £2 per week by bringing in snacks from home instead. But what if she forgot to bring a snack some mornings because she was late and in a hurry?

Rose's weekly budget		
Income	**Expenses**	**Goals**
Pocket money £5	Drinks and snacks: £2 After-school pizza get-together: £3	**Short term:** CD £15 Birthday present £10 **Long term:** Skirt £35 Shoes £40
Total income £5	**Total expenses** £5	**Total goals** Short term: £25 Long term: £75

Rose could also cut out the pizza get-together with her friends. But this was an important part of her week, and a chance to catch up with her friends outside school. She really didn't want to give this up.

Rose realized that in order to achieve any of her goals without either cutting down on her expenses or getting into debt, she needed to somehow increase her income. She quickly found a weekend babysitting job, earning herself an extra £15 per week.

Be realistic

Note that Rose thought about her expenses *realistically*. Giving up her weekly snacks and drinks is still an option she could choose to take – but she would need to remember to bring in snacks from home every day, However, Rose knew that giving up the weekly pizza get-together would make her feel she was losing touch with her friends. Her new job means that she can continue to enjoy these meetings and save money.

Rose's new weekly budget		
Income	**Expenses**	**Goals**
Pocket Money £5 Babysitting £15	Drinks and snacks: £2 After-school pizza get-together: £3	**Short term:** CD £15 Birthday present £10 **Long term:** Skirt £35 Shoes £40
Total income £20	Total expenses £5	Total goals Short term: £25 Long term: £75

Rose's weekly income is now £20. She continues to spend £5 per week on expenses, but her income is now £15 greater than her expenses. She is able to save her babysitting earnings of £15 per week (£60 per month), which makes her goals achievable.

A weekly job, such as babysitting, can make a real difference to your income.

THE SPENDER

Charlie is a Spender. He never seems to have enough money saved up for his goals, and always hopes that his parents will pay for everything. Unfortunately for Charlie, his parents will not buy him anything until his next birthday – which is six months away! Lately, Charlie has also been borrowing money from his older brother, just to meet his weekly expenses. He already owes his brother £60. What is Charlie going to do?

The first step is to make a budget so that it's easy to see what's going on. You can see Charlie's budget on the chart below.

Oops! This budget shows exactly why Charlie cannot save his money and needs to borrow **cash** from his brother. Each week, Charlie spends £16 but has an income of only £6. His expenses are significantly more than his income. This makes Charlie a Spender.

Charlie's weekly budget				
Income	**Expenses**		**Goals**	
Pocket money £6	Video games at the arcade	£5	**Short term:**	
	Pizza on Wednesdays	£3	Pay back brother	£60
	Ice cream on Thursdays	£2	CD	£15,
	DVD rental for		Video games	£30
	Saturday night	£4	**Long term:**	
	Snack machine	£2	MP3 player	£100
			Computer	£600
			Digital camera	£200
Total income £6	**Total expenses**	**£16**	**Total goals:**	
			Short term	**£105**
			Long term	**£900**

Charlie can only become a Saver by altering his approach to money. In other words, Charlie needs to decrease his expenses, or increase his income – or both.

Plan 1: Spend less!

Charlie could opt to spend less money each week. He could stop going to the video arcade after school and instead play video games at home with his friends. Charlie could also eat snacks from home, rather than from the school snack machine. Finally, Charlie could stop renting DVDs and either borrow them from friends, or settle for watching TV.

By opting for the Spend Less plan, Charlie would save £1 per week towards his goals – but it would take him a very long time to achieve them!

Plan 1: Spend less		
Total income	**Total expenses**	**Amount saved**
£6	£5	£1

Plan 2: Make more!

A second option could be for Charlie to increase his income by getting a job. It is spring, and he likes to be outdoors. So, he could look for a job mowing lawns. Charlie could earn himself as much as £25 a week with a new lawn-mowing job.

A new job would boost Charlie's income to £31 per week. Even if Charlie decided not to cut down his expenses (video games, pizzas, and so on) he could still save £15 per week towards his goals. So, Charlie would officially become a Saver!

Plan 2: Make more money		
Total income	**Total expenses**	**Amount saved**
£31	£16	£15

Mowing lawns is a good way to increase income.

Plan 3: Spend less and make more!

Charlie could decide to spend less money by cutting out video games at the arcade and not using the school snack machine. This would bring his total weekly expenses down to £9 per week. He could also decide to mow lawns for an extra £25 a week.

With his new weekly income increased to £31, and his new weekly expenses decreased to £9, Charlie's income would be significantly more than his expenses. He would have £22 per week to save towards his goals. Charlie would now be a Super Saver!

Plan 3: Spend less and make more!		
Total income	Total expenses	Amount saved
£31	£9	£22

• CHECKLIST •

1) Make a list of your weekly income. Try to include sources of income that you receive regularly, such as an allowance.

2) Then, make a list of your weekly expenses. Include expenses such as food and after-school activities.

3) Make a list of short-term and long-term goals. Which ones do you want to afford first? Prioritize them. Now, write down the costs of your goals.

4) Look at your income and your expenses. What is the difference between your weekly income and your weekly expenses? Do you have more income than expenses? Are you a Saver or a Spender?

5) If you are a Saver, how much money are you saving each week? How long will it take you to achieve your goals?

6) If you are a Spender, you need a plan to become a Saver. How can you spend less, make more, or do both?

7) Finally, review your budget often. If your income, expenses, or goals change, make a new budget.

Comparing the plans

Charlie has three options for turning himself into a Saver. But how does each plan compare?

Now try to work out how long it would take Charlie to pay back his brother and afford his other goals by adopting any one of the three saving plans outlined in this chapter.

Charlie's saving options			
Plan	Total income	Total expenses	Amount saved
1. Spend less!	£6	£5	£1
2. Make more!	£31	£16	£15
3. Spend less and make more!	£31	£9	£22

DID YOU KNOW?

In 2001 a woman in the United States named Eulalie M. Scandiuzzi invented moneyboxes called Moonjars to help young children understand their money choices. A Moonjar is a colourful cardboard box that is divided into three sections. These sections reflect the three choices for using money: saving, spending, and giving. Children can use Moonjars to keep track of how they use their money. The different sections of a Moonjar are divided as follows:

- **Save (blue):** for keeping money tucked away
- **Share (red):** for giving to a favourite charity
- **Spend (green):** for buying things that are needed and wanted

THE FAMILY BUDGET

Families also need to budget income against expenses and goals. For most families, the main source of income is parents' salaries. Housing is the main expense for most families. Clothing, food, and transport are also large expenses. If a family's income is more than its expenses, then the family is saving money.

Different families have different goals. Going on holiday, improving the house, buying a car, and saving money for university are all typical examples of family goals.

Think about your own family:
1) What is the main source of income for your family?
2) What are the main expenses in your family budget?
3) Finally, what are your family's goals? Write down your list of family goals. Next, ask your parents and siblings to make lists. Are your goals the same?

"Annual income: twenty pounds. Annual expenditure: nineteen pounds, nineteen shillings and sixpence.
Result: happiness.

Annual income: twenty pounds Annual expenditure: twenty pounds, nought and sixpence. Result: misery."

(Mr Micawber in David Copperfield *by Charles Dickens)*

This pie chart shows an example of how one family might spend its income. This family's largest expense is housing, which is fairly typical of most households in the UK. The family also saves 5% of its income.

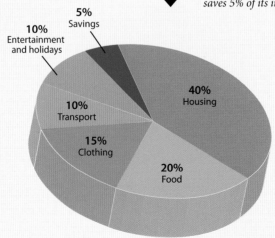

5%
Savings

10%
Entertainment
and holidays

40%
Housing

10%
Transport

15%
Clothing

20%
Food

AND PLEASE DON'T FORGET...

Throughout the world, and within your community, there are many people whose most basic needs are not being met. Local and worldwide charity organizations are working to alleviate many of these concerns, but they need help. The box on the right lists a few facts to get you thinking.

Just a pound a day

Did you know that in many parts of the world, less than £1 a day can provide a child with food, clothing, medical care, and education?
This proves that even quite small donations from ordinary people really DO make a difference.

Don't forget to do your part to help those in need. Try to make giving one of your regular money goals.

DID YOU KNOW?

- According to the international children's charity organization UNICEF, approximately 10 million children under the age of five die each year from deaths that could have been prevented with proper medical treatment

- UNICEF also reports that 115 million children worldwide do not attend school, mainly due to poverty.

- According to the international charity WaterAid, more than 1 billion people around the world do not have access to clean water).

Understanding Banks

The idea of a **bank** began in the 18th century BCE, when people kept various forms of money, including grain and gold, in temples for safekeeping. In the 4th century BCE, many modern-day banking practices, such as lending money, began in ancient Greece and Rome. But by the 1200s, Italy had emerged as a major banking centre.

money houses

Today, there are thousands of banks all over the world, and probably at least one near your home or school. A bank is a place where your money can increase in value, or grow. It is an institution where you can store your money. In future it may even enable you to borrow money to buy a house or a car.

Finding your way around

Inside a bank you will generally see a fairly large room. Behind glass security screens sit bank **cashiers** who help customers to put in or take out money. Banks also have separate areas where you can open accounts, obtain foreign currency, borrow money, or make **investments**.

Most banks these days offer accounts that are especially designed for students and young people.

BANK ACCOUNTS

Banks offer several types of account, including **current accounts**, **savings accounts**, **fixed rate accounts**, and **student accounts**.

Current accounts

To open a current account you must usually be at least 18 years old. A current account is different from a savings account. With a savings account, the bank pays more interest to account holders. With a current account, the bank pays less interest. A current account usually comes with a book of **cheques** and a **debit card** that you can use in a **cash machine** (see page 25.)

Savings accounts

Many children and teenagers open a savings account. Opening an account begins with putting in, or **depositing**, money in the bank. The bank pays **interest** to customers with a savings account. Interest is money earned on the amount of money in a bank account. (See pages 28 to 33 for more on interest.) So, the **balance**, or amount of money, in a savings account can grow through interest.

Access to the money in a savings account may be restricted. You will not be able to withdraw money using a cheque book or a debit card.

Fixed rate accounts

There is a special savings instrument called a **fixed rate account**. These earn even more interest than a regular savings account, because they offer higher interest rates. But they also require the deposited money to be kept in the bank for a certain length of time, such as a year or two. After the fixed period, the interest rate that relates to the account is usually reduced.

Student accounts

Student accounts are designed by banks especially for students. They are basically current accounts, so they come with a cheque book and a debit card, but they also have extra features to suit students. For example, they may have an agreed **overdraft** limit. This is an amount that the bank agrees to lend you, in addition to the balance in your account. Student accounts may also have more flexible terms.

DID YOU KNOW?

The word bank comes from the Italian word "*banca*", which means "bench". Hundreds of years ago, Italian bankers did their money lending from benches!

OPEMING A BANK ACCOUNT

Once you understand how banks and bank accounts work, it is time to open an account. Inside the bank there is usually an area for opening new accounts, where bank employees will help with filling out the forms. When opening a new bank account, you will need to:

- Remember to take along a form of personal identification, such as a birth certificate.

- Remember to take enough cash with you in order to make the initial deposit into the new account. This deposit is the account's starting balance. Some banks will allow a new account to be opened with as little as a £5 **deposit**, but it is best to check this with the individual banks first.

Choosing your account

Once the forms are filled in, the bank will provide details on how to manage your account. Depending on the sort of account you have opened, they will also issue you with the following:

- For a savings account, the bank will provide a book with the account holder's name and a new savings account number. They will usually give you a book of deposit slips so that you can deposit money into your savings account. (See page 24 for more about deposit slips.)

- For a current account, the bank will provide a cheque book with the new account number. A current account usually comes with a debit card to use for making purchases and for withdrawing money from cash machines (see page 25).

As a new account holder, you will also be asked to sign a signature card for security reasons.

When all this has been done, your new account is opened.

Using cheques

A cheque is a form of payment. It is a written set of instructions that tells a bank to take money out of an account to pay someone. Although nowadays more and more people use cards for purchasing, cheques are still an important and useful form of payment.

If you pay a friend with a cheque, your friend will then pay your cheque into his or her own bank account. Your cheque will take a few days to "clear", while your friend's bank checks with your bank that there is enough money in your account to honour your cheque.

This illustration shows how most cheques are laid out, and the correct way to fill one in.

If you want to use a cheque to pay for an item in a shop, you will also need a cheque guarantee card. This is the same as your debit card.

If there is not enough money in your account, your cheque may "bounce". Banks will usually charge for a bounced cheque, unless you have already arranged an overdraft (loan) facility with them.

A cheque shows the name and address of the branch of the bank.

On the top line write the name of the person or place that is being paid.

The date

BANK OF CORNWALL
LICHFIELD (309504) BRANCH

21-03-18
50826791

Date *10 July 2008*

Pay *Ron's Music Shop*   Only   £ *35 – 68*

Thirty five pounds and sixty eight pence

A/C Payee

ROBERT SMITH

Robert Smith

Check No.   Sort Code   Account No.

1⑆02697   21 03 18   50826791⑆

These numbers include the cheque number, the branch's reference number, and your account number.

The amount of the cheque must be written in words on the second and third lines, and in numbers in the box.

A cheque is invalid unless it is signed!

USING DEPOSIT SLIPS

The bank will also issue you with deposit (paying-in) slips. These will either be inside your cheque book, or in a separate booklet. Deposit slips are used to pay cash or cheques you have received into your bank account.

The illustration shows how most deposit slips are laid out, and the correct way to fill one in.

The date is written on this line.

The name of the account holder is written here.

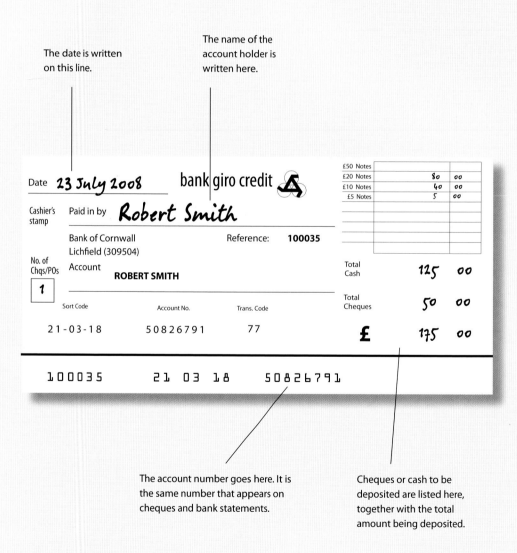

		£50 Notes		
Date **23 July 2008**	bank giro credit	£20 Notes	80	00
		£10 Notes	40	00
		£5 Notes	5	00
Cashier's stamp	Paid in by **Robert Smith**			
	Bank of Cornwall Lichfield (309504)	Reference: **100035**		
No. of Chqs/POs	Account **ROBERT SMITH**	Total Cash	**125**	**00**
1		Total Cheques	**50**	**00**
	Sort Code Account No. Trans. Code			
	21-03-18 50826791 77	**£**	**175**	**00**

100035   21 03 18   50826791

The account number goes here. It is the same number that appears on cheques and bank statements.

Cheques or cash to be deposited are listed here, together with the total amount being deposited.

24

The debit card

A debit card has a magnetic stripe, also called a magstripe. The stripe consists of small iron-based particles, which contain information such as the issuing bank's name and a **Personal Identification Number (PIN)**. A PIN is a string of numbers linked to a particular card. The debit card can only be used with the correct PIN number.

The cash machine

A cash machine is exactly what it sounds like – it dispenses cash automatically. Cash machines are accessible 24 hours a day and seven days a week. They are connected to the bank's central computer. A debit card allows a cardholder to use a cash machine to withdraw money, or to check the balance in his or her bank account.

DID YOU KNOW?

On 27 June 1967, the first cash machine in the world was installed in Barclays Bank in England. By the end of 2005, approximately 1.5 million cash machines were found across the globe. By 27 June 2007, £26 billion was dispensed from them worldwide. Cash machines can be found almost anywhere in towns and cities. A person with a bank account in London can **withdraw** money from a cash machine in Beijing, China – all because of modern technology!

People can withdraw their money at any time of day or night using a debit card in a cash machine.

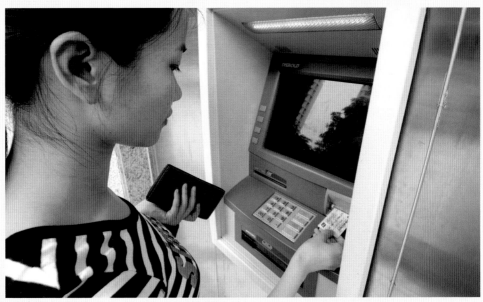

KEEPING TRACK

It is important to keep careful track of the money in a new account. The bank sends statements to account holders. A bank statement covers a certain period of time (usually a month). It lists a beginning balance, an ending balance, and any deposits or withdrawals that were made to the account during that period. It will include any payments that were made by cheque.

These statements are proof of payment. They show that a cheque payment was made and was received. Account holders can check the statement with their cheque book to see if the balances match up.

Cash machine records

A receipt can be printed when a cash machine **transaction** is finished. This receipt is a record of the transaction. You can also print out a note of the available balance in the account. With a withdrawal, the money is automatically taken out of the account, so the note shows the balance with the withdrawal. But if you have made a very recent deposit, the available balance will not necessarily include the transaction.

Another way of keeping track of your spending is by filling out the Transaction/Payments Record form inside your cheque book. You will find these slips either at the front or at the back of your book. The illustration below shows you a typical example.

A transaction record helps you to keep an eye on your spending.

Date	Details	Money out	Money in	Balance
25/5/08	Dick's Stores	£15.97		£165.06
26/5/08	Bike shop – inner tube	£6.99		£158.07
30/5/08	Morris Music – CDs	£20.08		£137.99
1/6/08	Mrs Smith: Babysitting		£40.00	£177.99
2/6/08	Pet Supplies	£35.92		£142.07

QUIZ

FINDING THE RIGHT ACCOUNT

This quiz will help you determine which bank account is right for you. Answer the questions by choosing the best response.

1) If you wore a T-shirt that best described you, what would it say?
   a) Super Saver
   b) Big Spender
   c) True Budgeter

2) You look in the window of the music shop and see a new CD from your favourite group. Your friends urge you to buy it. What do you do?
   a) Wait until you earn enough money to buy it
   b) Run to the nearest cash machine
   c) Think about it, and then head to the bank and withdraw money to buy the CD

3) You are given a gift of cash by a favourite aunt. What do you do with the money?
   a) Invest it all into a high-earning savings account
   b) Blow the whole amount on a big party for your friends
   c) Spend some of it on new clothes and music and lock the rest in a drawer

4) What is your attitude towards money?
   a) A penny saved is a penny earned
   b) Money in my hand is money spent
   c) Money helps me meet my needs

See page 50 to find out the answers.

27

Understanding interest

The concept of **interest** can seem very confusing. But it is actually quite simple – and it is the main way that **banks** make their money. As you will discover, interest can earn you money too!

Simple interest

If a customer wants to borrow money from a bank, he or she must pay interest to the bank for the loan. Interest is a small percentage of the total value of the loan. However, if a customer saves money in the bank for a period of time, he or she will earn (be paid) interest from the bank. The banks use some of the interest they have earned from the borrowers to pay interest to the savers.

Simple interest is when the bank pays money to customers as a percentage of their original balance. A bank may offer an **interest rate** of 10 percent. This means a customer who has £100 in this bank would receive 10p for each pound per year. At the end of the year, the customer would have £110, provided that he or she did not take out or put in any more money.

Interest rates make a difference

The amount of interest that a customer receives depends on the bank's rate of interest. The higher the interest rate, the more money a customer makes.

Joey opens a bank account with £1,000. He does not put in or take out any money during the year. But Joey still makes money because the bank pays him interest.

However, the amount of money that Joey makes depends on the bank's interest rates.

Here is what happens to Joey's money with different interest rates:

Joey's original balance	The bank's interest rate	Interest earned	Joey's new balance at the end of the year
£1,000	5%	£50	£1,050
£1,000	10%	£100	£1,100
£1,000	15%	£150	£1,150

- At an interest rate of 5 percent, Joey would receive £50 in interest at the end of the year.
- At an interest rate of 10 percent, Joey would receive £100 in interest.
- And if the interest rate is 15 percent, Joey would receive £150 in interest.

At the end of the year, Joey has more money in his bank account because the bank has paid him interest. Joey earns the most interest with the highest interest rate.

Balances make a difference

The amount of money that someone has in the bank is called a balance. Since the interest that someone earns is a percentage of the balance, different balances earn different interest payments.

Joey puts his money in a bank that has a 10 percent interest rate. He does not put in or take out any money during the year.

- If Joey put £50 in the bank, then he would earn £5 in interest.
- If Joey put £100 in the bank, then he would earn £10 in interest.
- If Joey put £200 in the bank, then he would earn £20 in interest.

Joey earns the most interest with the highest original balance. So, the higher the original balance, the more interest is earned.

Here is what happens to Joey's money when the interest rates stay the same, but his original balance changes:

Banks often post their interest rates for savings and overdrafts in their windows. Different banks may have different rates. This is because banks use their interest rates to compete with each other for customers.

Joey's original balance	The bank's interest rate	Interest earned	Joey's new balance at the end of the year
£50	10%	£5	£55
£100	10%	£10	£110
£200	10%	£20	£220

COMPOUND INTEREST

Compound interest is the money that a bank pays customers on their original balance *and* on their interest earned. Here is how compound interest works.

Joey opens a bank account with £1,000. The bank pays Joey 10 percent interest. During the first year, Joey does not take out or put in any extra money. At the end of the first year, Joey earns £100 in simple interest, and his new balance is £1,100.

But what happens in the second year? Joey's beginning balance in the second year is no longer £1,000. It is now £1,100. So, Joey earns interest on his original balance of £1,000, plus he earns interest on the extra £100 that he received in simple interest.

Joey's balance grew even faster with compound interest than with simple interest. This is because compound interest means receiving interest on the original balance *and* on the interest already earned.

Year	Joey's beginning balance	Simple interest earned on original balance	Joey's new balance with 10% simple interest	Interest earned on simple interest money	Joey's new balance with 10% compound interest
Year 1	£1,000	£100	£1,100	£0	£1,100
Year 2	£1,100	£100	£1,200	£10	£1,210
Year 3	£1,210	£100	£1,310	£21	£1,331
Year 4	£1,331	£100	£1,431	£33.10	£1,464.10
Year 5	£1,464.10	£100	£1,564.10	£46.41	£1,610.51

Compounded often

Banks can compound interest annually, meaning once a year. They can also compound interest daily, weekly, monthly, or every four months. Account holders earn more money when the compound interest is paid more often.

Simple interest	Compound interest
Calculated as a percentage of the original balance	Calculated as a percentage of the balance and interest already earned
Calculated once a year	Can be calculated several times a year

INTEREST AND LOANS

Keeping your money in a bank can *earn* you interest. But a bank can also *charge* you interest. Because many people keep their money in banks, banks have a lot of money. Banks use this money to make **loans**. Loans allow people to borrow money. When people take out a loan, they can pay it back bit by bit (in **instalments**), or all at once.

Interest-free loans

Jonathan wants to buy a computer for £600, but he cannot afford it. So Jonathan borrows £600 from his brother to buy the computer. Now Jonathan owes his brother £600. Jonathan and his brother work out a plan for Jonathan to repay the loan.

Jonathan cannot afford to pay back the £600 all at once. However, he can afford to pay his brother £150 per month. In four months' time, Jonathan has repaid the £600 debt to his brother. This is called an "interest free loan", because Jonathan's brother has not charged Jonathan any interest on the loan.

Interest is one way to make your money work for you.

Twins Amy and Ozzie each received £100 for their birthdays. Amy deposited her £100 in a savings account that offered an interest rate of 10 percent compounded quarterly, or four times a year. Ozzie put his gift safely in his sock drawer. At the end of the year Ozzie still had £100 tucked away in his sock drawer. But Amy now had £110.38 – her original gift of £100 plus £10.38 earned in compound interest.

Month	Jonathan's monthly payments	Amount that Jonathan owes his brother
May		£600
June	£150	£450
July	£150	£300
August	£150	£150
September	£150	£0

Interest on borrowing

In the example of Jonathan and his computer, Jonathan paid back the £600 that he borrowed. But in real life a bank, and other organizations will charge a price for lending money. This cost is also called interest. In this case, interest is the cost of borrowing money – as a percentage of the original loan amount. The more money borrowed, the more interest paid. When people have fully paid off a loan, they will have paid both the amount of the original loan and the interest owed.

The cost of a bank loan

When money is put into the bank, the customer receives interest. When money is borrowed from the bank, the customer pays interest.

The following example is typical of a university student's loan experience:

Sara borrows £1,000 from the bank to help pay her fees. The bank charges her 10 percent simple interest, so each year Sara owes another £100 in interest. Sara agrees to pay back the money in three years.

Year	Sara's original loan	Total interest that Sara owes the bank	New amount that Sara owes the bank
Year 1	£1,000	£100	£1,100
Year 2	£1,000	£200	£1,200
Year 3	£1,000	£300	£1,300

Even though Sara borrowed £1,000 from the bank, she owes the bank £1,300 by the end of the third year. For Sara, the cost of borrowing money is the extra £300 in interest that she owes the bank.

Security

Banks use the money they make from interest to make loans. This does not mean that when people want to take money out of an account, the money may not be available because someone else is using it.

The amount of money you have in your bank account (the amount on your bank statement) is *your* money. The banks are obliged by law to return it to you whenever you want it.

Banks are the safest place to keep money. They have fireproof vaults with a lot of security. However, very occasionally banks do get into trouble and run out of money. Fortunately banks also have government insurance, so that each bank account holder is guaranteed to receive a certain amount of their money if the bank gets into trouble.

Deposits are protected under the Financial Services Compensation Scheme (FSCS). Since 1 October 2007, the scheme provides 100 percent protection for up to £35,000 per customer if a bank or building society is unable to pay claims against it.

THE INTEREST CYCLE

1. CUSTOMERS DEPOSIT MONEY

2. BANKS USE MONEY TO MAKE LOANS

3. BANKS RECEIVE INTEREST PAYMENTS ON LOANS

4. BANKS PAY INTEREST TO CUSTOMERS WITH BANK ACCOUNTS

5. CUSTOMERS' BALANCE GROWS

6. BANKS USE MONEY TO MAKE LOANS

DEBIT AND CREDIT CARDS

With the use of cash and cheques decreasing in the 21st century, debit and credit cards have become the preferred methods of payment. Many banks and financial companies issue both types of card.

DEBIT OR CREDIT CARDS?

Many people use **debit cards** to pay for their purchases. These cards are like cash or a cheque because they take money directly from a cardholder's bank account at the time of the transaction. A debit card only allows people to spend up to the amount in their account. If people try to use their debit cards to spend more money than they have in their account, the transaction is declined by the bank.

Credit cards

In the United Kingdom, most adults own at least one **credit card**. A credit card is a way to borrow money. Credit card companies give a spending limit to each credit card holder. This credit card limit is the full amount that a person can borrow from the credit card company. A company determines the credit card limit for cardholders by working out how likely people are to pay their bills.

Cards are now the most popular method of payment.

DID YOU KNOW?

Most shops accept credit cards and debit cards for making purchases. It is usually better to pay with a debit card than a credit card, if you have the money in your account, because payments with a credit card may incur interest.

Credit cards may allow people to spend more money than they have in their bank account. This is because using a credit card is like using money from a loan. A credit card company loans cardholders up to the amount that it believes credit card holders can eventually pay back.

Getting the card

People who apply for a credit card fill out a form with their name, address, and financial information. Before offering credit, the card company will want to know about the applicant's payment and credit history. Most credit card companies do not offer credit cards to children under the age of 18. As well as banks, building societies, and other financial institutions, many large shops issue credit cards.

Performing the transaction

Credit card transactions are not automatically withdrawn from a person's bank account. When a person uses a credit card, the credit card company pays for the purchase. The credit card holder pays back the credit card company later.

Credit card holders receive monthly statements from the card company. This states the minimum amount the card holder should pay each month, (and by which date) and the amount of interest charged.

Paying the bill

Credit card holders often have the opportunity to pay back the credit card company in two ways:

1) Credit card holders can pay off the full amount owed to the credit card company in one payment.

2) Credit card holders can pay a minimum balance per month, which is a percentage of the full amount. For example, if someone owes £200, he or she might pay £25 in monthly instalments until the debt is paid off.

Facing the consequences

If people cannot pay the full balance each month, the credit card company charges them interest on the remaining balance. Many credit card companies charge higher interest rates than banks charge for their loans. People who borrow money with a credit card and cannot pay the full balance will owe more than they originally spent.

A Vicious Cycle

Being allowed to spend more money than we have can sometimes lead to debt. Credit card debt is a terrible cycle faced by many people around the world. It involves being unable to pay credit card bills and owing more money each month because of compounded interest and late fees. In 2006, there was £220 billion in credit card debt in the United Kingdom. So how does a person get into this mess?

Owing more

In May, Heather received a credit card bill of £1,100, but she could only pay back £100. So Heather still owes the credit card company £1,000. The credit card company charges 18 percent interest on all unpaid balances. Heather also did not pay her bill on time. The following month, Heather did not use her credit card. How much does Heather owe in her next statement?

You can see from the statement below that Heather owes £205 *more* than she did last month, because of the interest charged and the late fee.

DID YOU KNOW?

The average consumer in the United Kingdom has debts of just over £3000, and this figure is rising. The most expensive debts are those on store cards. About 16 million Britons owe a total of almost £2.2bn on store cards. The average interest rate charged on these debts was almost double the average interest rate on other credit cards.

If Heather cannot pay £1,205 she will owe even more money next month. This is another example of compound interest – but working against the credit card holder this time.

The amount of interest that Heather owes compounds each month. If Heather continues not to pay her full balance, then growing balances and compounded interest payments will lead to credit card debt.

Heather's statement			
The remaining balance that Heather owes the credit card company	18% interest charged by the credit card company on the unpaid balance	Late fee charged by the credit card company	Heather's new balance
£1,000	£180	£25	£1,205

How are some tips to avoid the credit card trap:

TIP

1) Do not use credit cards as a form of payment. Debit cards and cash allow people to spend only what they have in their bank accounts.

2) Make a budget to determine sources of income and expenses. Put monthly credit card payments at the top of the list of goals. How much money can be used to pay the credit card debt? Is it possible to increase income and to decrease expenses in order to have more money available to pay off the debt?

3) Make a list of credit cards and amounts owed on each card. Many people in credit card debt own more than one card. In the United Kingdom, the average adult has five cards! Next, list the interest rates of each card. Pay off the credit card balances with the highest interest rates first.

4) Consult a professional. There are organizations that help people in credit card debt. These places can make plans to repay debt in manageable instalments.

There are professionals who help those in credit card debt. Services can be provided in person, online, or by phone.

CREDIT OR DEBIT CARD?

	Advantages	Disadvantages
Credit Card	1) They are lightweight and easy to carry. 2) They allow the purchase of goods or services without carrying around a lot of cash. 3) If the bills are paid on time, they can yield a good credit history. One day, a good credit history may help with buying a house or a car. 4) Credit card companies often compete for customers by offering special deals. These deals may include allowing a credit card holder to have an "interest free" year. During this time, a cardholder is not charged any interest on unpaid balances. 5) They are accepted as payment in most places. 6) They can be used to make in-store or online purchases.	Credit cards have many disadvantages, including: 1) the temptation of convenient spending 2) swiping a card allows people to spend up to their credit card limit, whether or not they actually have this amount of money in their bank account 3) if people cannot pay their balance, they will soon have to pay back their balance *and* the interest charges 4) other problems include high interest rates and the chance of growing debt.
Debit Card	1) They are lightweight and easy to carry. 2) They allow the purchase of expensive goods or services without carrying around a lot of cash. 3) They do not come with a bill at the end of the month. 4) They only allow people to spend what they have in the bank, limiting the chance of debt. 5) They are accepted in more places than cheques. 6) They can be used to make in-store or online purchases.	Debit cards also have a few disadvantages: 1) you can only withdraw money you have in your account up to your overdraft limit 2) there is less protection with a debit card than with a credit card. If a debit card is lost, someone can use it to withdraw money directly from the cardholder's account

Getting it
Wrong

Julia was excited when her new credit card arrived in the post. The credit card company had given her a £500 credit card limit! Julia mistakenly thought that the credit card company had given her £500 to spend. She ran off to buy the latest mobile phone – complete with a camera, text messaging, and Internet access for emailing. Then Julia used her new phone to call friends and ask them to join her for lunch – her treat! By the end of the day, Julia had blown the whole £500. When Julia arrived home, her mum asked her how she had paid for the phone and lunch. Julia told her about the credit card. Her mum quickly explained that Julia had to pay the credit card company back, or risk owing them more money. Julia was very upset. How was she going to come up with £500 to repay the credit card company?

QUIZ

CREDIT CARD QUESTIONS

Are you credit card savvy? Or are you likely to get into credit card debt? Take this quiz and find out!

1) While out shopping with your friends, you find a shirt that looks great. As you do not have any cash, you plan to pay by credit card. You:
   a) buy one in every colour
   b) buy just the shirt you tried on
   c) walk out of the store.

2) Your new credit card came in the post and you have a credit card limit of £500. You:
   a) run to the shops and buy £500 worth of clothes, music, and food
   b) buy just the new CD that you wanted
   c) tuck the card away in your wallet for a rainy day.

3) Your friends are trying to convince you to buy a new video game. You have your credit card. But you do not have the money in your wallet or in your bank account to cover the cost. You:
   a) buy the video game anyway. After all, you have a whole month to work out how you are going to pay for it.
   b) tell your friends to buy it for your birthday
   c) leave the shop and forget about the game.

4) While visiting your brother at university you notice groups of people trying to get new students to sign up for credit cards. You:
   a) advise your brother to get as many credit cards as possible. The more cards he has, the more credit he has to spend
   b) ask your brother about the pros and cons of a credit card
   c) suggest going for pizza

See page 50 to find out!

STOCKS AND BONDS

Stocks and bonds are another option for your money. They are types of investment, and they give investors the opportunity to make money.

WHAT IS A STOCK?

A **stock** is a part of a company. A person who owns a stock, called a **stockholder**, owns a share in the company. Companies issue different quantities of shares. If a company issues many shares, each share is probably only worth a small part of the company.

Shares cost money. Different companies have different share prices. The price of a company's shares is determined by many factors, including company performance, world events, and the level of demand for a company's product.

A risky investment

A stock is a type of growth investment. People invest their money in stocks because they hope that their value will increase, or grow, over time. When the value of a stock increases, stockholders can make money when they sell their shares. If stockholders buy a stock for £10 each and the share's value increases to £15, they will make a profit of £5 per share when they sell them.

Owning stocks can be a risky investment, because the potential profit is constantly changing. This happens because share prices change. When a stock's price decreases, investors can potentially lose money. However, if a stock's price increases, investors can potentially make money.

The rule for profitable stock investments is: buy low, sell high! Stock investors will make money if they buy the shares at a low price and sell them at a high price.

Dividends

Stockholders can make money without selling their shares when they receive **dividends**. A dividend is a share of the company's profit given to the stockholders. However, not all profitable companies pay dividends.

Why do companies issue stocks?

Stocks are a source of income for a company. When people buy shares, they pay the company that issued them. A company can then use this money to run their business.

*Stocks are bought and sold each day by **brokers** at a place called a stock exchange. There are many exchanges throughout the world, including the London Stock Exchange, the New York Stock Exchange, and the Tokyo Stock Exchange (below).*

Each year a company releases an annual report to its **shareholders**. This report tells the shareholders about the company's income, expenses, and goals.

Finding stocks

People keep track of stocks by reading newspapers or using the Internet. Financial pages list many individual stocks. These listings include the company's ticker symbol. This symbol is a combination of letters that represent a particular stock. For example, the ticker symbol for the Microsoft Corporation is MSFT.

A stock listing includes the dividend per share, and how much the stock is worth at the end of the day. It will also show the change in a share's value from the close of the previous day's trading to the end of the current day's trading. It is this change that allows shareholders to make money, or that warns them about losing it.

How to get involved

Here are some investment tips:

- Think about the things that you and your friends buy and do. For instance, is there a popular brand of trainer? What about a favourite place to eat? Stock prices are driven up by an increase in demand for a product. Maybe the things that you like are also things that many teens across the country enjoy. Check out the companies that make these products.

- Follow a stock over a few months by studying the newspaper or the Internet. Are there any trends in the share price? Is the stock's value increasing?

- Read a company's annual report. This shows a company's performance and future plans.

- Think about your goals for a stock investment. How long are you planning to keep the shares? Do you want to use the expected profits to meet one of your short-term or long-term goals?

BONDS

Bonds are another type of investment. A bond is a loan to a government or a company. People who buy a bond receive interest on the loan. A fixed bond specifies a fixed interest rate, also known as a fixed rate of return. A bond has a **maturity** date, which informs investors when their initial investment will be repaid.

Melissa's investment

Melissa buys a £1,000 five-year government bond at a 10 percent fixed rate of return. Interest is paid yearly.

Year	Investment made by Melissa	Interest earned at 10%	Money paid to Melissa at the end of the year
1	£1,000	£100	£100
2		£100	£100
3		£100	£100
4		£100	£100
5		£100	£1,100
Total	£1,000	£500	£1,500

Melissa makes an initial investment of £1,000 when she buys the government bond. She receives £100 in interest payments each year. At the end of five years, the government repays Melissa her initial £1,000, and Melissa has earned £500 in interest payments.

Less risk

Buying bonds is considered less risky than buying stocks for many reasons. First, bondholders are repaid their initial investment when the bond matures. Secondly, many bonds have fixed rates of return. Thirdly, companies that issue bonds put up **collateral** to secure the loan. For example, if a bond-issuing company loses its money, it can sell its buildings, computers, and other assets to repay the bondholders. Government savings bonds are a safe investment because they are backed by a country's government.

Getting it Right

In 1999 three teenagers from Illinois in the USA started a website called TeenAnalyst. com. that teaches young people about the stock market. It also tracks stocks in products that may be familiar to young investors.

You can follow the performance of stocks and shares by reading the financial sections of the newspapers.

WHAT KIND OF INVESTOR ARE YOU?

Take this quiz to find out what kind of investor you are.

1) While checking your email, you read a pop-up about a stock that is on the rise. You:
   a) convince your mum to buy the stock
   b) follow the stock for a week
   c) close the browser and start emailing

2) Your grandmother gave you a £100 for your birthday. You want to invest in the stock market. You:
   a) buy a stock whose company made the front page
   b) buy a stock that was recommended by your dad
   c) change your mind and blow the £100 in the shops

3) It is the summer holidays and you earn £75 babysitting some local children. You:
   a) immediately find an investment with a high rate of return
   b) buy a bond with a fixed annual interest payment
   c) treat yourself to an item off your list of goals

4) You are a contestant on a TV show. The banker has just offered you £150,000. You can take the deal now, or you can try for a higher offer. If you continue, you have a 35 percent chance of making up to one million pounds. But you also have a 65 percent chance of being offered less than £150,000. You:
   a) try for the million pounds
   b) take the £150,000
   c) wake up, because it is all a dream

See page 50 to find out what kind of investor you are!

TIPS FOR SPENDING LESS

There are many traps that can easily lead to overspending. By recognising these traps before you hit the shops you can avoid falling into them.

PRESSURES ALL AROUND

Friends can pressure other friends into buying things. But friends (even a best friend) may have different budgets, different spending habits, and different goals. Always stick to your own budget and do not allow peer pressure to persuade you into spending more than you can afford.

Advertising

Companies spend a lot of money on advertising. Adverts try to convince people to buy a product. Advertising is all around us – in print (catalogues, newspapers, and magazines), and on television, the Internet, even mobile phones. The online advertising market in the United Kingdom was worth almost £3000 million in 2007.

Companies know that advertising sells. But, are you always willing to buy? An advert tries to persuade you that you need a product. But most of the time, you only want it. Before you buy anything you see advertised, ask yourself, "Do I really need this item?".

Getting it Wrong

Maya and her best friend, Janet, are shopping in town. Maya's mum gave her £100 to spend, while Janet's mum gave her £25. When the friends pass by Gotta Have Clothes, Maya sees a hot pink, £15 T-shirt in the window. She runs in and buys it. Maya also convinces Janet to buy the same T-shirt.

At Must Buy Boutique, Maya sees a matching sweater and a cool pair of jeans. She pushes Janet to buy those, too. Janet knows that she does not have enough cash, but she does have her credit card.

"I saw your favourite singer wearing these jeans in a magazine," urges Maya. "Soon everyone in school will have a pair. Imagine being the first to wear them!" Janet finally gives in and buys clothes that she cannot afford.

Ads for goods and clothing often feature celebrities. But shoppers should remember that they are not buying a celebrity's way of life. They are only buying the item for sale.

Smart shopping

Being a smart shopper helps a person to spend less money. **Comparative shopping** can often result in the best prices. Most items are sold in different places, including department stores and online shops. Sometimes one shop will charge less for the same item than another shop – so it pays to make the effort to shop around!

Shopping online can often work out cheaper, too. But always check with your parents before buying anything on the Internet. When ordering online, remember to add the delivery cost to the price of your goods.

Sales

Sales are good for consumers. In the sales, prices are reduced. For example, a coat that cost £150 might go on sale for £75. What a bargain! Also, consider looking in second-hand shops for "good as new" clothes, books, and other items.

Coupons

Think about collecting coupons. A coupon is a piece of paper that reduces the price of an item, or offers the buyer a better deal. Coupons can be found online, in newspapers, in catalogues, or in the shops. They usually have expiry dates, so use them while you can.

To sum it up

Good money management can make the difference between feeling relaxed, in control of your life, and able to achieve your goals – or stressed out, worried, and out of control! Try to get into good money habits as early as possible, and you will never regret it!

Plan a budget

Get into the habit of budgeting. This means making a regular review of your income, your expenses, and your money goals. Make yourself a spreadsheet (see examples on pages 12–14), and check it weekly. Be sure to include everything on your sheet.

Set realistic goals

Be clear about your money goals, and the difference between a need and a want. When listing your goals, be realistic about their order of importance. For example, it is always more important to repay a debt than to treat yourself to that new CD! Also, be realistic about how long it is likely to take you to afford your goals. This is important for items such as birthday presents that need to be bought by a certain date.

What are your choices?

Think carefully about your spending choices, and try to be firm with yourself. For instance, do you really need that T-shirt? Can you afford to buy it as well as, say, your weekly drinks and snacks? If not, are you prepared to go without the drinks and snacks in order to have the T-shirt, and not get into debt? Always try to ask yourself these sorts of questions before you buy anything.

Spend less make more

Think of ways that you can spend less, and make more:

- Are there any non-essential expenses you could cut out, or cut down? Maybe you buy too many fizzy drinks? If you only bought them once or twice a week, instead of every day, they would feel more like a treat – and you would save money!

- Ask your parents about little jobs you could do locally. Or perhaps you have a talent for making things that you could sell? Selling goods or services is an excellent way to boost your income. The fact that you have used your own **initiative** to earn money will also impress your future employers.

Hmm ... which will it be? The affordable shirt? Or the designer model? Spending money involves making realistic choices!

Be a smart saver

Make your money work for you. Ask your parents about opening a savings account. Be sure to do your research and find the account that offers the best rate of interest on your savings. You can do this online, in newspapers, or at the banks themselves.

Investing

If you are interested in stocks and bonds, start learning more about them now. Your teacher or librarian may be able to recommend books or websites where you can find out more about financial systems.

Careful with those cards!

There is no doubt that credit cards can be a useful tool when used sensibly. BUT remember that the money is a loan, not a gift, from the credit card company! The loan must be paid back in regular instalments. Failure to do so can result in the credit card company charging large amounts of interest – and an uncontrollable debt. Credit card repayments should always be included in any budget plan.

And finally ...

Remember that you have three choices when it comes to using your money: you can spend, save, and *give*.

QUIZ RESULTS

FINDING THE RIGHT ACCOUNT
For page 27

- **If your answers were mostly a):** You have a mature attitude to spending and saving. You can handle both kinds of account.

- **If your answers were mostly b):** Looks like you still need to think more before you spend. Stick to the current account for now.

- **If your answers were mostly c):** You like to save, but you are not making your money work for you. Try a savings account.

WHAT KIND OF INVESTOR ARE YOU?
For page 45

- **If you answered mostly a):** You were made for the stock market – but take care that you don't get too carried away!

- **If you answered mostly b):** You are a careful investor – a mix of stocks and bonds may be the way to go!

- **If you answered mostly c):** You should stick to a bank account, and be sure to budget wisely.

CREDIT CARD QUESTIONS
For page 40

- **If you answered mostly a):** You could be in major danger of credit card debt. Get a grip on your spending – now!

- **If you answered mostly b):** You think before you spend, and will make a responsible credit card user.

- **If you answered mostly c):** You are as credit savvy as they come. Keep it up!

20 Things to Remember

1. Know the difference between your needs and wants. Thinking of everything as a need can quickly lead to overspending.

2. Remember that you have three money choices: save, spend, and give. Donating money to a worthy cause can make a difference.

3. Make a budget that includes your weekly income, weekly expenses, and goals.

4. Prioritize your goals and make a plan to achieve them.

5. Review your budget – income, expenses, and goals change.

6. Understand your family's budget – it affects you.

7. Open a bank account. Start saving and make your money grow with interest.

8. When opening an account, ask questions. The more you know, the more money you can make.

9. Shop around for the bank that offers the highest interest rates. The higher the rate, the more money you will earn.

10. Remember that you need to have money in the bank to earn the interest. Making an initial deposit and then spending all the money will not earn you interest.

11. Using a debit card adds up. Keep a record of your transactions.

12. Be careful with credit cards! Swiping means borrowing money that you have to pay back.

13. Beware! Credit card debt happens faster than you think.

14. Remember that stocks and bonds can earn you money. They often give higher rates of return than a savings account.

15. Do the research on stocks – they carry risk.

16. If the value of your shares increases, remember that you need to sell the shares to make a profit.

17. Parents and teachers are great resources to learn about current investment opportunities. Ask them your questions.

18. Do not give in to peer pressure. Respect that you and your friends have different budgets.

19. Buy what you need, not what the adverts make you think you need.

20. Be a smart shopper – comparative shop, look for sales, and use coupons.

Further information

WEBSITES

This website is packed with simple, clear, independent information about money:
http://www.moneybasics.co.uk/

Credit Action is a national money education charity and its website will tell you everything you are looking for about managing money:
http://www.creditaction.org.uk/

This website of the Bank of England has lots of information on the history of banknotes and how they are made today:
http://www.bankofengland.co.uk/banknotes/index.htm

This is the website of the Royal Mint, where you can find out all about how British coins are made:
http://www.royalmint.gov.uk/Corporate/BritishCoinage/british_coinage.aspx

BOOKS

Smart Money, Danielle Denega (Scholastic, 2008)

Money: Earning, Saving, Spending, Margaret C. Hall (Heinemann, 2007)

Rich Dad, Poor Dad for Teens: Money, What You Don't Learn in School, Robert T. Kiyoshi and Sharon L. Lechter (Little Brown, 2004)

The Teenager's Guide to Money, Jonathan Self (Quercus, 2007)

Big Money, Little Effort: A Winning Strategy for Profitable Long-Term Investment, Mark Shipman (Kogan Page, 2008)

FURTHER RESOURCES

Parents and teachers are also resources. Talk to them about money and how to save, spend, and give. Bank employees can answer questions and provide explanations about banking transactions and accounts. Your school may also have a programme to help you learn about managing money.

Disclaimer
All the Internet addresses (URLs) given in this book were valid at the time of going to press. However, due to the dynamic nature of the Internet, some addresses may have changed, or sites may have changed or ceased to exist since publication. While the author and publishers regret any inconvenience this may cause readers, no responsibility for any such changes can be accepted by either the author or the publishers.

Glossary

balance amount of money in a bank account

bank place that stores money and valuables, increases balances, and makes loans

bartering trading

bond loan to a government or a company that pays back an initial investment with interest

broker someone who buys and sells stocks and bonds on behalf of clients

budget plan that lists income, expenses, and goals

cash actual money, either paper money, or coins

cashier person who serves the public in a bank

cash machine machine that dispenses cash and balance statements

cheque piece of paper that tells the bank to pay someone money from a bank account

collateral borrower's property promised to the lender in the event of a loan default

commodity good or service

comparative shopping comparing the prices of an item

compound interest interest as a percentage of the balance and the interest already earned

credit card plastic card used for spending that allows someone to borrow money from the company that issued the card

currency money, including paper money, and coins

current account bank account that gives customers cheques and a debit card to use

debit card plastic card that acts like cash or a cheque

denomination different value of money

deposit put money into the bank

dividend part of a company's profit paid to the shareholder

expense item that is bought

fixed rate account savings account that pays interest at a slightly higher rate for a given period of time

goal something that it is desirable to achieve

income source of money

incur to cause to happen to oneself

initiative ability (or boldness) in beginning or taking on new projects

instalment one of a series of regular money payments made over a period of time

intaglio method used to make paper money

interest money earned on the amount of money in a bank account

interest rate percentage of a balance that a bank pays a person, or a percentage of a loan that someone owes the lending company

investment something that a person puts money into, with the intention of making money or a profit

loan borrowed money, often from a bank or other financial institution

maturity end of a specified period of time, such as in a financial obligation

mint place where coins are made

need item required for survival

opportunity cost what someone gives up in order to buy something else

overdraft when you have spent more money than you have in your bank account

personal identification number (PIN) string of numbers that allows a person to use a cash machine card

savings money that someone does not spend or give away

savings account bank account that pays a higher rate of interest than a current account

shareholder person who owns shares in a company

simple interest interest earned on an initial deposit

stock share of a company

stockholder person who owns part of a company

student account bank account especially for students

transaction activity that involves banking, such as making deposits and withdrawals

want something that a person desires to have

withdraw take out money

Index